Values and Purpose Workbook

Companion Book to

The REAL Purpose-Driven Life

By Robert Villegas

The Values and Purpose Workbook

Companion to The REAL Purpose-Driven Life

By

Robert Villegas

www.robertvillegas.com

robertv1989@outlook.com

ISBN-13: 978-1544638324

ISBN-10: 1544638329

Published in the United States of America.

Series Title: Villegas Self-Improvement Volume 4

Social Media Addresses

CloutHub @RobertVillegas

WimKin Robert Villegas

MeWe Robert Villegas

Minds @Robertv1989

Gab @V4Vendata

Dedicated to My Father

Robert Regino

Table of Contents

Introduction

This book is based upon my book *The REAL Purpose-Driven Life* which spells out a unique approach to pursuing life's purpose. It is intended to function as a workbook which will help you work through the issues of developing your values and purpose. It is published for your Kindle (or tablet) device so you can type your ideas and thoughts as you go through your daily activities. At points where your input is requested, you can use the comment feature of your device.

I am going to provide a clear workbook here that focuses on the steps of the process discussed in the wider book. I would suggest you read the original book before you start working through the value steps. It will give you a better foundation for understanding what you want to make of your life.

This workbook can also be handed out to patients by counsellors and psychologists to provide material for counselling sessions and even group discussions for people who are dealing with psychological problems that impinge upon moral issues and values.

Enjoy the journey.

Step 1. Leading with your Mind

The first step involves getting your mind under control so it can make correct decisions for you.

In order to properly direct your life, you must become an independent thinker. I'm talking about doing the best you can to think with your own mind rather than follow what you are told by authority figures, peers, parents and other family members.

The key to starting this intellectual liberation is to do an assessment of how independent you are in making your own decisions. Here are a few questions to ask:

1. Do you often change your mind or feel uncomfortable when someone disagrees with you or criticizes something you do?

Notes:________________________________

____

____

____

____

____

____

____

____

2. Is your first thought on any issue what other people think rather than what you think?

Notes:

3. Do you prefer to investigate an issue and study it to define what you think – or do you just ask others?

Notes:

Thinking for yourself first is not an easy habit to create. It requires some basic knowledge of how good thinking is done and even a little courage. You can start by reading some introductory books on logic or clear thinking.

My favorite book on logic is "Elementary Lessons in Logic" by W. Stanley Jevons. This classic may be hard to find but there are other good books. I would suggest you start with basic thinking and avoid, at first, the more advanced treatments that will confuse you. One book that I like is "Thinking as a Science" by Henry Hazlitt which can be found on Amazon.com. Here is the paid link to this book: http://amzn.to/2jNN93H

Thinking for yourself is essential to defining your purpose and values. And you will find it to be enjoyable. Try to convert your discoveries into actions by writing them down for now.

Notes:____

Step 2. Experience What You Already Know

We must start at fundamentals and *the* most fundamental concept is what you already know. You must learn to consistently and fully accept the things you already know. For instance, when you accept what you already know, you accept the law of identity (the idea that things are what they are and they act according to what their nature).

This acceptance of what you already know should be more than just a neutral statement. You must see the connection between knowledge and your life directly in everything around you. You must connect your mind efficiently to reality. This is, or should I say, this should be the goal of every human being who wants to be moral.

This exercise will help you as you think through your values and move toward your purpose in life. I have written below a list of different perspectives on established. Read through each of them and contemplate their meaning and importance.

Write down your thoughts as you ponder each perspective and see what you can learn from each of them:

- The basic principle of the universe is existence. Reality is immutable, things are what they are, they are part of one whole and all entities in the universe operate according to the same set of universal principles.

Notes:________________________________

- The purpose of human consciousness is to understand existence. We can be certain of what we see, and in areas where abstract reasoning is required, logic and the principles of induction apply. Certainty and confidence in the human mind are the results.

Notes:

- The idea that existence exists is the starting point, the foundation upon which life and happiness proceed. In order to deny existence, one has to use it as part of the denial – in other words, one has to accept existence in order to deny it.

Notes:________________________________

- Previous knowledge creates a core for certainty and benevolence. The harmony, the consistency and the certainty that come from the idea that reality is what it is, that things are what they are and that it is in their natures as entities to do what they do, will bring peace of mind and a core sense of life that will carry you to the next stage of intellectual development and set the stage for reason, purpose and self-esteem.

Notes:______________________________

- Reason will be the method through which you will develop, grow and achieve understanding of both previous and new knowledge.

Notes:________________________________

- Existence is everything around you and you must understand that it is everything. You must ensure that this principle is part of every thought you have about reality.

Notes:

- Everything is existence and when you are consciously aware of it, your mind is clearer. Everything you see, don't see, everything around you, every person – everything is existence. Existence is everywhere and everything. There is nothing else.

Notes:

- Existence is eternal – it will stand for all time, and this is a magnificent source of wonder – the acceptance of this reveals that the conscious mind cannot get around or under existence. There is no such thing as magic. You can only love something that exists or that existed. You cannot love or feel anything for non-existence because it does not exist. Nor should you fear non-existence. How can you fear something that does not exist?

Notes:________________________________

- Existence is immutable. You can't change it with a wish. You can only act to change something in existence or influence others to think and act. Once something has happened, good or bad (in terms of human value judgment), it has happened. You cannot change it. This is also magnificent because this fact is the source of certainty (not uncertainty as mystics claim). It is also the source of human feeling which can only be about things in existence. You can't love that which has never existed, is nothing and has never been anything. You can only love things in existence. Values are part of existence and they relate only to you and your life in this universe – nowhere else.

Notes:_______________________________

____

____

____

____

____

____

- You may be able to affect the future of existence in some ways, but you cannot change what has happened. You must accept it. This principle exposes the true power of existence and its complete primacy in man's mind. You cannot change the past. You can only make the future by living in the present. That requires the use of your mind focusing on reality and action that is sufficient to the accomplishment of your chosen values.

Notes:__________________________________

- Existence is metaphysical – this means it is everything in reality. It is all of reality and you only understand it as a metaphysical fact of existence.

Notes:

- Existence is not ruled by a consciousness, it cannot be forced by a mind, by the will, or by chance. You must accept what is but it is better to focus more on the good that is. This means the emphasis should be on the positive rather than opposition to the negative (to non-existence).

Notes:____________________________

- Existence and knowing the real is what enables man to survive. It helps him live well and longer and healthier and more productively. Existence and knowing the real is the only way to live a good life. This is the most positive idea that man has ever come up with (existence) because his acknowledging it gives him everything good (for life) that is possible. It is not important to dwell on the negative arguments against existence when there is so much positive about it that man should celebrate and worship. This positive argument is all you need to deal with the negative arguments that are untrue.

Notes:________________________________

____

____

____

____

____

____

____

- In this sense, the world is not going to change rapidly. A good estimate is that about 90 percent of your present knowledge won't change at all for the rest of your life. What will change is the amount of new usable and beneficial knowledge you gain. There will likely be no "bad" knowledge that turns your world upside down because most of it is metaphysical in nature, unchanging, and the man-made (even) was built by men who knew the nature of reality when they made it; so, if anything, your knowledge will likely increase due to new knowledge and very little upturning of old knowledge. This is because existence is necessary for survival (it must be consistent) and it is consistent (metaphysical) and unchanging. There is very little to be insecure about regarding the idea that the world is changing too rapidly for you to survive well. It is not changing that rapidly in the more "solid" sense. Life will always continue to get better. This is good news.

Notes:________________________________

- Existence is ruled by the law of identity which holds that every existent has a nature, and it must act according to that nature. This is why existence cannot be changed to any appreciable degree. The laws of identity and cause and effect apply universe-wide in places you will never go, see or know about. One minor man-made change here on earth does nothing to the overall scheme of the universe which operates according to the law of identity. You are safe. This is more good news. There is no need for insecurity.

Notes:________________________________

- Always trust your body. You were designed for survival by millions of years of evolutionary development. Don't think that your body will not work hard to keep you alive. It is designed for success.

Notes:

- Nature is outside the power of will. It simply is “nature”.

Notes:______________________________________

- Consciousness can only observe, judge and think/learn about existence (and only existence).

Notes:

____

____

____

____

____

____

____

- In reality, because one can't merely wish for things to happen, only rational action will make anything happen. This is because you must first use your mind (reason) to decide how to make a specific value come about. Then you must act in such a way that the value will be brought into existence. Values cannot be created in a vacuum. You can only take steps toward the accomplishment of values, and for this you must wait until you have done the correct thinking, taken the appropriate actions, and then secured the value as your own.

Taking steps such as earning money, planning how the value will look and what it will do. Once the tools and resources and plans are in place, you must purchase and/or create the values you want and then secure it to yourself or exchange it for other higher values that you can offer in trade. For this reason, values should never be taken away from you once you have earned them.

Notes:______________________________

- Values are "values". They cannot be cavalierly taken away. It is evil to appropriate any value because it dismisses all the thought and action taken to acquire it and it diminishes human valuing. Wishes won't make it proper to re-distribute anyone's values.

Notes:

- On the other hand, once you realize you do not possess (at the present time) a particular value, you cannot wish the value to be delivered immediately. You must take certain steps to acquire it. You must be patient enough to know that wishing does not make it so; you must plan and wait. There are no enemies here keeping their values from you. There are only the "requirements of reality" which can only be dealt with through long-range thinking and action.

Notes:______________________________

- Existence is the metaphysically given. The metaphysically given simply is. You can make judgments about existence but you cannot alter the nature of existence. The metaphysically given is the standard of judgment. "To rebel against the metaphysically given is to engage in a futile attempt to negate existence. To accept the man-made as beyond challenge is to engage in a successful attempt to negate one's own consciousness. Serenity comes from the ability to say "Yes" to existence (to love it and value it). Courage comes from the ability to say "No" to the wrong choices made by others."[1] (parenthesis mine)

Notes:______________________________

____

____

____

____

____

____

____

[1] The Metaphysical versus the Man-made by Ayn Rand

- Nothing is exempt from, nor can it violate, the law of identity. Rand holds that everything that is (that exists) is subject to the law of identity and the law of cause and effect. It is what it is, past, present, future. It can't be wished out of existence.

Notes:_______________________________

- Consider the implications. Among other things, you are not exempt from the law of identity. You have capabilities, needs, and a volitional form of consciousness which are part of your identity. Likewise, nothing you do is exempt from the law of identity. Therefore, other men are not to be feared or capitulated to. They are to be judged for their rational or irrational actions. They should never engender fear. They are responsible for all they do – you are not required to obey them, pander to them or give in to them. As a rational person, you can see the potential value in all men and therefore if you love the reasoning capacity of man, you need not fear men. That gives you the self-confidence to deal with them without fear. Love replaces fear of people because you can't fear someone or something you love.

Notes:______________________________

- Reality does not think and creates no "God" for you to worship, the least of which includes the opinions of others. Others are not gods. Faith is a dependency on the minds of others. Giving in to others is a matter of faith. Reality is not amenable to emotions and thoughts while people are not immutable and unquestionable.

Notes:

- The man-made is also part of existence once it has been made – but it can be judged, evaluated, changed, improved, destroyed and corrected. The man-made is the province of man; but to create the man-made, man must perceive, evaluate, judge, identify, conceptualize and then act upon his knowledge of existence. His correct judgment is not the metaphysically given; it is the only thing that enables creation for man. It is the only thing within his control.

Notes:

Step 3. Experience Your Own Existence

You must experience your own existence by grounding it in reality. You must know yourself as clearly and consistently as possible. You will learn a lot about existence, but the key principle of existence is that it is you who lives in the real world. Below you will find a list of "truths" about your own existence. Go through this list and write down what it means and how each of them relates to you as a person living in the world:

Some facts about your existence:

- You exist
- You are part of the universe
- You have rights; freedoms that derive solely from existence
- You are one and indivisible
- You have the right to participate in this universe
- You are an individual
- You are connected mentally only to yourself
- You are a sovereign and autonomous human being
- You exist in the world
- You can survive only by means of your mind

- You love existence
- You love reality
- You love your mind
- You love your values
- You love reason, rationality and self-esteem
- You act for your own wellbeing
- Reason is your prime capacity
- You have the right to your independence
- You have the right to your production (property rights)
- You are alive
- You have the right and responsibility to define your own values
- You have the right to pursue your purpose in life
- Your thinking belongs only to you
- Your mind's purpose is to correctly ascertain reality
- You have a right to be happy
- You have a right to be moral and do the right thing

Notes and Comments:

Notes:________________________________

____

____

____

Step 4. Learn to Stay Positive

All negative concepts are connected by a common aversion to life and an adherence to the idea of death, loss and stress. Once you recognize this principle, you will be able to develop an antipathy toward the negative which can only lead to an acceptance of the positive/the good/peace of mind and happiness.

Too often, we allow the negative to intrude into our characters. Your goal should be to turn all negative thoughts into positives. It starts with the physical aspects, the tensions, doubts, psychological land mines and philosophical traps that society has imposed upon you. Yet, you have the ability to win; but winning means defeating the negative. Winning is a positive.

The goal here is to weed out every aspect of negativity from your mind and its effects on your body. The negative is unhealthy while the positive is cleansing and healthy.

Each of these characteristics below posits the broad principle of life versus death. You can go on incessantly dealing with each individual instance or you can integrate them into a broader abstraction and get a better fuller understanding of the principles involved. This chart helps you be stronger in fighting the negatives which are listed on the right-hand column. By keeping yourself striving for the positive, you can achieve the overall goal which is to live positively, healthily and morally. As you go through the list, write down your thoughts about the two opposites (positive/negative) and ask yourself why is the positive attitude good and how does the negative attitude harm you. Connect these traits to reality by asking yourself what actions reflect the positive and the negative.

Here is a clue to evaluating negative attitudes. First, we tend to resist negative thoughts and feelings (physical tension) so we don't have to think about them. This is called denial. But denial makes the negative feeling or attitude stronger and gives it a firmer grip on your mind. The secret is that resisting a negative is not the way to stop being negative. The way to stop being negative is to focus only on the positive and identifying the emotional benefit of the positive, arguing for the good that is in the positive and thereby contrasting positive and negative so you can choose to be positive with conviction.

You will find that this process will give you a stronger respect and appreciation for the positive in life. It enables you to see positive and negative as reality-based and gives you a stronger conviction that the only way to look at life is to be positive, to have good expectations. This also has many benefits for your overall wellbeing and state of mind. It will establish a stronger frame of reference for evaluating reality and it gives you a better view of life overall.

Life	Death
General Disposition	
Positive	Negative
The basic positive attitude requires reason and a focus upon reality. The primacy of existence is the idea that existence is primary and that understanding the nature of existence, the real, is paramount in having a positive attitude. Notes:________________	The negative is a focus on the zero, death, un-being, nothingness – there is no argument for it. Notes:________________

Light	Darkness
A metaphor that connotes positivity	A metaphor that connotes negativity
Notes:____________________	Notes:____________________

Peace of Mind – no worry about the future	Panic – always worry about what will happen
Peace of mind comes from certainty about metaphysical reality. Existence Exists.	The future is uncertain because the mind is uncertain. The Supernatural can lead to doubt and fear.
Notes:______________________	Notes:______________________

Love of Mankind	Anger and Conflict with other men
This is a general view of man's nature. Is he good or evil by nature? If you think he is good by nature you are prone to have better relations with people.	If you think men are evil by nature or weak, you will find lots of conflict with others and even yourself. Confusion is the result.
Notes:__________________	Notes:__________________

Hope for good	Dread/Despair about the future
Hope is positive, an expectation that good will happen if one thinks and acts out of positive notions Notes:____________________	This is anti-hope, the opposite of positive expectations. It is a very powerful force that suppresses happiness Notes:____________________
Optimism Optimism is another term for hope but more certain of a good outcome Notes:____________________	Pessimism Another term for despair but more philosophical as it is supported by a general sense of reality Notes:____________________

Metaphysics

Existence	Non-existence/Nihilism (Primacy of Consciousness)
How to tie the positive to existence: Understand that existence is the real and you can only be positive bout what you know with certainty. Certainty is knowing reality/existence. Existence has primacy – but more than this, it is. Notes:____________________	Non-existence has no relation to existence/reality. It is a negative concept and the negative does not exist and one should learn that it has no presence in reality and in the mind. Non-existence "is" "non", it has no presence in reality. Notes:____________________

Science	Mysticism
Science is the study of existence. It is based on the primacy of existence. Existence is the only presence, the only reality and in logic that means A is A. Notes:____________________	Mysticism is the contemplation and adherence to non-existence. It is the essence of negativity and is based on the false premise that consciousness, by itself, is the only reality. It is the practice of non-existence, the negative. Notes:____________________
Truth/Good Epistemology Truth can only be found by connecting concepts to existence. This is done by the	Falsehood (False Characteristics create False Concepts Falsehood comes from bad epistemologies that lead to lies

individual defining his concepts according to accurate "defining characteristics" Notes:	or mistakenly defined characteristics of things and/or adherence to them through false premises. It can lead to false notions and eventually nihilism. Notes:

Knowledge	Ignorance
Knowledge results from good epistemology, good/true concepts which leads to true identification of reality and correct action based on reality.	Ignorance is the opposite of knowledge. It is based on bad epistemology, concepts wrongly defined which lead, in action to poor decisions.
Notes:____________________	Notes:____________________

Primacy of Existence (Objectivity)	Primacy of Consciousness (Mysticism)
Objectivity means being objective which means being correct about reality. This leads to correct decisions. The goal of thinking positively is to know existence.	The Primacy of Consciousness is dependent upon the thought (of man or god); that the thought creates reality. It leads to epistemological "anything goes" types of thinking.
Notes:____________________	Notes:____________________

A is A	A is Non-A
A is A means existence exists. A thing is what it is. It is the essence of metaphysical certainty.	This is the contradiction, the lie, the falsehood, the evil, the malicious, the hateful and destructive; nihilism.
Notes:________________	Notes:________________

Logical	Illogical
Takes A is A and applies it consistently to all thinking. Notes:____________________	Rejects A is A and seeks a none-standard that leads to anti-mind and anti-man thinking Notes:____________________
Truth Truth = objectivity Notes:____________________	The Irrational and Untrue Truth is rejection of existence, the non-standard, the non-real, the non-man, the zombie Notes:____________________

Reason	Mysticism and Irrationality
Logic and objectivity applied to all thinking from A is A to the widest abstractions.	Logic is just a different opinion that has equivalence with mysticism.
Notes:	Notes:

Reality	Supernatural
A synonym for "Existence", reality refers more specifically to the world of things and anything which is said to exist. Notes:	A world presumed by mystics to exist outside of the natural world. It describes the essence of mysticism and religion, a false concept that has not been "proven" to exist. Notes:

Morality	
Self-Interest When the individual puts his/her own interest first, it is because he wants to advance a positive sense of living. Existence must be acknowledged and the existence of the individual requires the life of the individual as the highest standard that leads to the highest level of success. Notes:____________________	Altruism Altruism denies that the individual should be first in his own life. It is anti-mind and anti-man. It is based upon envy and hatred of the good. Notes:____________________

Concerned about Positive Values and Achieving them	Concerned about what people/altruists think or do
Positive values are based on the standard of life. They lead to life and are based upon love of existence which is the source of all life and happiness. Notes:______________	Negative values are focused on the secondary on the views of others and therefore are disconnected from existence. They are haphazard and eventually destructive. Notes:______________

Values	Nihilism
See above Notes:____________________	Nihilism is the desire to destroy values. It is anti-values intent, not on ignoring positive living, but on an active effort to destroy all values. It is essentially hatred of human striving and flourishing. Notes:____________________
Individualism This is the valuing of the individual in his or her living.	Collectivism This is the avoidance of active living by negative thinking.

Notes:	Notes:
Active Living See above. This is the development and active pursuit of values by means of integrating action to the goal of value pursuit. Notes:	**Depression and Doubt** This is the avoidance of active living by negative thinking. Notes:

Personal Situation	
Freedom of Action	Tension
Only a rational person, one connected to reality, can be free to act rationally. Notes:	The negative person is not free to act rationally. He has no order or consistency because he is not connected to reality. His actions are controlled because that is the only action he can take. Notes:

In Charge of Your Life Requires life-serving decisions and actions. Requires reason. Notes:____________________	Life is Controlled by others Requires altruism and collectivism, dependence and inability to make life-serving decisions. Notes:____________________

Liberty	Fight/Flight/Freeze
Liberty refers to the freedom you have to make your own decisions in life and to live for your own self-interest. Notes:____________	The restriction of liberty (within the individual) is the response to fear of the opinions of others as they relate to your personal choices. Altruism is the source of these opinions of others. Notes:____________

Grounded	Uprooted
Grounded in reality. Conceptual with good concepts. Notes:__________	Separated from reality as is all mysticism – and anti-conceptual mentality. Notes:__________
Happiness	Depression
The successful state of life when the mind is connected to reality and integrated with the body and its needs. Notes:__________	The failed condition when the mind is disconnected from reality by negative and faulty thinking methods and rationalizations. Notes:__________

Solid Personhood	Vulnerable
Habitual reliance on reason builds a solid person. Reason is the source of human power to affect reality in order for man to survive well.	Vulnerable to the vicissitudes of reality-cause and effect because weak or disconnected from reality. Vulnerable to evil men because one does not know they must be fought.
Notes:____________________	Notes:____________________

Independence of Mind and Ideas	Dependence of Mind and Ideas
Reason can only come from an independent mind. Notes:____________________	The mind mired to dependence upon the ideas of other people will always be dependent. Notes:____________________

Living This is the ultimate choice that guides all thinking and acting. Notes:___	Dying The opposite (negative) of living. Notes:___

Thinking	Brooding
True thinking is focusing on reality which yields tangible positive results and confidence. Notes:______________	Brooding is negative thinking about something wrong and negative emotions of anger and futility. Notes:______________

Consciousness	Unthinking and Unconsciousness
Consciousness of reality means a positive view of "what is". It is a process for knowing not for making reality.	Unthinking is relinquishing the responsibility. Unconsciousness is the absence of focus and unthinking about the real.
Notes:______________________	Notes:______________________

Mindfulness	Refusal to Think
The ability to use your mind in a self-directed way that will positively affect your life. Notes:______________________	The conscious choice to let emotions guide your choices, sometimes automatized and automatic after a time. Notes:______________________
Mind/Body Unity	Mind/Body Split
When mind and body are seen as a unit, there is no conflict and the individual functions more efficiently to the individual achieves happiness. Notes:______________________	When mind and body are split, there is conflict, disorder and unhappiness. Notes:______________________

Winning at Life	Losing at Life
Good values, good actions = love of life = happiness.	Disvalues, wrong actions = hatred of life = unhappiness.
Notes:______________________	Notes:______________________

Objective Philosophy	Immanuel Kant
Objective reality – Primacy of Existence.	Primacy of Consciousness – Duty.
Notes:__________________	Notes:__________________

Full Relaxation Stress-free living – moral living, primacy of existence, peace of mind, integrated mind and body. Notes:________________	Unease and High Blood Pressure Immoral living, primacy of consciousness, out of context thinking, concrete-bound thinking, nti-conceptual mentality, dis-ease, mental disorder. Notes:________________

Healthy Eating	Unhealthy Eating
Count calories, sugar, cholesterol, sodium, etc. And eat right. Notes:__________	Eat to die, eat to make you feel better, to avoid life. Notes:__________
Happiness/Moral Living Defining values and making rational choices = happiness. Notes:__________	Immoral Living Having no standards of value. Making decisions emotionally = unhappiness. Refusal to think = misery. Notes:__________

Creating	Destroying or Not Creating
Creating requires combining the parts of reality for life-enhancing uses. It requires knowledge of reality, imagination and integration as well as value-definition.	These require nothing and lead to depression and unhappiness. They lead eventually to "acting out" and nihilism.
Notes:	Notes:

Exercise/Activity	Sedentary/Inactivity
Keep energy flowing. Keep life flowing. Keep body active and efficacious.	Give life away. Cease activity. Give up. Die.
Notes:	Notes:

Organization of Life Focus on values and goals with life as the standard. Keep a written record of your values and order them hierarchically. Notes:	Disorganization and Unconcern about Life Floating through life. Give little thought to values. Ignore goals and plans. Notes:

Know that metaphysical world is not conscious	Think that physical reality is a thinking entity
Accept the real and that it is the only universe but it operates according to its nature and has no thought of choice.	Mysticism – Reality is conscious – the world's worst and most dangerous concept. Reality does not think or act or choose.
Notes:________________	Notes:________________

Judge the man-made	Fear men and what they do
This is an issue of justice and identifying whether the acts of people are positive or negative. Notes:______________	Fear of the thoughts of men and the refusal to judge represents and inordinate amount of fear of human consciousness. It implies the Primacy of Consciousness. Notes:______________
Competence (in myself)	Incompetence (in myself)
An active mind, practiced in reason, will achieve competence and moral acumen. Notes:______________	An inactive mind is an insecure mind. Notes:______________

Doing the right thing The right thing is the moral thing. It requires looking at reality and thinking, the result is happiness and satisfaction. Notes:	Doing the wrong thing Refusal to think leads to doing the wrong thing and leads to failure and unhappiness. Notes:

Admiration of competence in others	Inefficacy in others
This is a matter of justice – knowing of good and rewarding it.	Results from not thinking clearly or refusing to think. Admiring inefficacy is nihilism.
Notes:	Notes:

Reward value Justice for the good is more important than punishing the evil. Notes:__________	Reward disvalue Rewarding disvalue is the opposite of justice and harms the good. Notes:__________

Romantic art	Naturalism
Romantic Art reflects human values and is on the positive side. It reflects the human drive to achieve the highest value. The drive for values is the drive for life.	Things as we happen to find them and the acceptance of human weakness is negative because there is no drive toward values and life.
Notes:__________________	Notes:__________________

Rational	Irrational
The rational mind is consistent in its adherence to reality. To be rational is to be correct.	The irrational avoids reason and is therefore wrong and failed.
Notes:________________	Notes:________________

Conceptual Definition accuracy Clear, precise definition mean clear, precise thinking. Not all concepts are created equal. Is there an issue you are dealing with that conceptual clarity can help you with? Notes:___________________	Conceptual Land Mine (poorly defined characteristics of concepts) Conceptual moral equivalency is a mixture of vague concepts with clear concepts – sloppy thinking. Moral travesty is thereby enabled. I call this the mixed economy of human thought. Notes:___________________

Cognitive Precision	Cognitive Imprecision
Concepts are unities of consciousness of reality. They are how I see. Their precision determines my accuracy of learning reality. Notes:____________________	Poorly defined concepts are the cause of failure and understanding. Notes:____________________

Integration of Knowledge	Disintegration of Knowledge
Since reality is an integrated whole, knowledge must be integrated with other knowledge. This yields full understanding. Notes:____________________	Mis-integration is the splitting or separation of non-knowledge. Mis-integration is "knowledge" based on mysticism and/or rationalism. They destroy man's focus (or scatter it) on reality and his acquisition of consistent knowledge. Notes:____________________

Integration of Knowledge	Mis-integration of Knowledge
Same as above.	Mis-integration is the splitting out of non-knowledge. Mis-integration is "knowledge" based

Notes:	on mysticism and/or rationalism. These concepts destroy man's focus (or scatter it) on reality and his acquisition of integrated knowledge. Notes:

Objective knowledge	Intrinsic knowledge
When knowledge is objective, it is based on verifiable knowledge. Checking the correctness of one's concepts is key. Notes:____________________	When knowledge is intrinsic, it comes from the emotions and characteristics of entities without abstract concepts. I represents concrete feelings assigned as characteristics of entities. Notes:____________________
Truth	Contradiction
Truth is the expression of what is real and actual. Notes:____________________	Contradiction is the expression of what is not real or actual. Notes:____________________

Objectivism This is a philosophy based upon the view that the human mind functions properly (or efficaciously) upon its evaluation of reality as it is. Notes:	Empiricism and Skepticism This is a philosophy that declares the human mind incompetent to ascertain and know reality. Notes:

One Reality	Two Realities
This view is the only axiomatic view, therefore the only view that leads to understanding and certainty.	Multi-views unprovable (un-validated) leads to confusion and doubt.
Notes:	Notes:

Morality of Living - Selfishness One must start with the self. This is the only way to moral living. This does not mean disliking others or being harmful to others. It means living. Notes:___________	Duty (Morality of Dying) Duty is the morality of dying. Notes:___________

Personal Hygiene	
Shaved	Unshaved
Notes:	
Well-groomed	Scruffy/Dusty
Notes:	

Bathed	Unbathed
Notes:______________________________	

Teeth Brushed	Teeth Un-brushed
Notes:______________________________	

Physical Health

Exercise Daily with Weights	Skip Exercise with Weights
Notes:______________________________	

Walk Daily	Skip Walk

Notes:

Yoga Daily	Skip Yoga

Notes:

Meditation Daily	Skip Meditation

Notes:

Smiling/Laughing	Frowning/Crying

Notes:

Healthy-range Blood Pressure Under 120/80	High Blood Pressure (Above 140 Systolic)

Notes:

Relations with Others	
Trust Recognition that there is Nothing to Fear from People – Love of People – Expressing Love or Appreciation to People – Thinking Positively about People Notes:	Prejudiced Fear of People/Need to Escape – Thinking that I Don't have the Energy for it – Wanting to Get Away from Them Notes:

Cooperating	Fighting

Notes:

Loving	Hating

Notes:

Speak truth and know the lie/untruth	Fear people and their opinions regardless of rightness or wrongness of them

Notes:

Additional Attitudes

Life	Death
Notes:	Notes:

Additional Comments:

Notes:

There are good influences in society and there are bad – but the responsibility to "get it right" is yours alone.

You are responsible for yourself. If you make a mistake in thinking, you will also make a mistake in acting. You must get the correct perspective and it starts with values.

The REAL Purpose-Driven Life is all about values, and not about faith and sacrifice. Values are the fundamental motivators of life. They take you to your purpose which is the ultimate value. However, the values you choose must be the right values; values that connect you to reality and make your purpose possible. Remember, values are based upon the standard of life; your life. Now we will engage in a process that helps you define your values, organize them and appreciate their importance for you.

Before we proceed, a short note:

The previous version of this book asked the reader to take out a piece of paper and make a list of their most important values. Since then, I have written a new book titled "EGOnomics – Finding your Full Ego" that provides a newer approach compared to that provided in the original version of this book. I have decided to supplement the approach previously taken with this new approach. The new text is below:

(The below text is copyrighted 2023 by Robert Villegas)

The Full EGO – How do we get to it?

The full ego is the realm of human action expressed by the individual who recognizes the importance of the ego in his life. The full ego is animated by the centrality of the ego in the individual's mind (Stage 1). The full ego (Stage 3) is rationality in action. It comes after the individual defines his values (Stage 2) and begins to apply his virtues.

I define the "full ego" as a realm in which most of man's moral choices are undertaken exclusively with "life as the standard". The connection between the individual's mind, his concepts, and reality has direct bearing on both the quality of thinking and on the results. When the human being, the individual, arrives at this realm of thinking, he/she does so volitionally after having discovered the primacy of the ego in Stage 1. He/she learns that if the ego is going to impact human life, a process of thinking, logic, so to speak, is required. The likelihood is that this choice was first undertaken (explicitly) by Aristotle, the first real intellect who lived among humans.

Aristotle showed that human thinking was an art, that it required hard work and clearly defined concepts. He taught that man must learn and develop a rational approach to the attainment of moral knowledge. It is likely that Aristotle did not see the full potential of human thinking; it may have been implicit in the practice of logic that he presented to his students.

In fact, Aristotle's presentation did not present the full picture regarding human thinking and only left us part of the full argument. He did not offer, as his first principle, the practice of induction (which would have been a major advance for human beings) that would have averted many of the disasters we have experienced over the last few centuries. What was explicit with Aristotle was his exposition of the practice of deduction that required correct premises for a successful syllogism.

The absence of induction, in Aristotle's teaching, is responsible for our present state of knowledge and the reason many men are mired in confusion and despair. The result is that men have been bamboozled by altruism and its anti-mind philosophy. They have no ability to live fully rationally. They are incapable of achieving their full ego, which is the ego at its best. The full ego requires proficiency at advancing self-interested action through effective strategies based on a fully defined value system (a code of values). The key for the individual is to recognize that the full ego is full rationality and moral knowledge.

It can be difficult to arrive at the state of the full ego because there are so many issues involved. These issues include:

- Accepted previous knowledge.
- The ability to "read" reality or evaluate it to connect the mind to it, and thereby develop a base of moral knowledge.
- The reduction of conceptual knowledge to the perceptual level.
- The ability to recognize when one has a solid base of moral knowledge.
- The ability to gage/measure moral knowledge on a consistent basis.
- The ability to monitor every moral decision made by the individual.

- The ability to judge the effectiveness/results of moral decisions.
- The ability to judge moral decisions that advance life as the standard.
- The ability to ascertain when moral choices are wrongly based on altruism or moral compromise.
- The ability to judge when one is operating on mixed moral premises/compromises with altruism, collectivism, social mores, and other irrational demands.
- Understanding how to identify rationalism in human thought and when you are thinking rationalistically and how to correct it.
- The ability to learn the difference between objective reality, Platonic/religious dualism, and Kantian/Humean rationalism.

One reason people don't understand their personal egos (or the concept of egoism) is that the ego is thought to be a negative. Because of this, the ego is virtually ignored by the proponents of religion and modern philosophy. This means most people are discouraged from seeking their egos or even learning how the ego is derived in a realistic sense. This causes them to openly ignore the facts that validate the ego and its primacy. The very idea of using logical evaluation (induction) to identify the existence of the ego is seldom considered important enough for a "good" person to ever want to do.

It is time to begin the process of understanding and validating man's ego. Moving from the centrality of the ego to full egoism will help the individual understand how to strive for it and how to become fully moral. Through a rational approach to the ego, we remove magic, miracles, pseudo-science, and indeterminacy from human living.

The self, of course is who you are. But more importantly, your perception of your self is the critical factor that affects behavior and tips the scale for or against successful living. If you hate your self because of common attitudes, you will immerse yourself in self-hate. On the other hand, experiencing full egoism requires first discovering the ego, loving the ego-centric attitude without guilt, and then making all moral decisions under the protection of reason.

Additionally, achieving a high level of egoism means the individual has learned the absolute importance of reason. No one can be right at all times, especially in a time when irrationality and indeterminacy are considered superior to rationality. This last is the mistake we need to eliminate from human thinking.

The full ego is an abstraction that starts with induction of the primacy of the ego and integrates it with the principles required for the development of a moral code and then the implementation of that code through rational action. The first question is "is there an ego and what does its existence mean?" This is Stage 1, and we will discuss it more fully later in this book.

Notes:____________________________________

Stage 2 is what happens when we have validated the existence of the ego. It involves defining and validating one's values and purpose in life while Stage 3 involves the actions the individual takes to accomplish his purpose utilizing the premise of "life as the standard". Once the individual becomes proficient at implementing his "plan" for his life, he arrives at the full ego.

Measuring the full ego can be a daunting task because it is difficult to know when one has arrived there. One can measure the rate of success or the percentage of success (coming from one's actions) and these can help. To a large extent, this measurement must be left up to the individual to determine for himself. To leave the effort to scientists or psychologists could expose us to the pitfalls of psychologizing which is largely a pseudo-science.

One can arrive at the psychological boundary marking the full ego by turning the study over to the field of moral philosophy which ties the ego to moral thought, and confines the ego to what the individual thinks and does. This study enables a "scientific" approach to moral decision making and gives man more confidence in his ability to be moral. Yet, in effect, the decision about when or how one arrives at the full ego (full morality) should be left to the individual.

Discovering your full ego and the importance of it for your life requires a logical, rational process of scientific induction. Yet, you cannot arrive at your full ego until you validate the primacy of the ego in all matters, and not before you create and validate your moral code.

This inductive approach to discovering your ego is not an emotional process. It is a rational examination of your inner core, the centrality of your personhood within the context of both your metaphysical and epistemological premises. Only on this foundation, can you begin the process of creating your moral code.

Your ego must first be discovered. In a sense, this is where Aristotle should have started. He should have shown that your moral code cannot be created without the foundation of the centrality of your ego. Your discovery of your ego is your discovery of the nature of the "you" as it exists in reality, it is your knowledge that your mind is competent to discover and choose moral action, and how you use your mind to act in reality.

Your ego is your isolated self; your *full* ego is your ego operating in reality. Your decision to use these broad concepts will help you create (or define) your moral code, your self-esteem, your widest purpose, and your effort to accomplish that purpose is of critical importance for your life.

Another aspect of the process of moving from your ego to your *full* ego is the early discovery of a concept called "the primacy of the ego. This primacy refers to the question of human value, specifically of your value, and in particular, the discovery that your ego is the center of your own personal perspective, of the centrality, objectively, of you as an individual. Once you reach the primacy of the ego, nothing can stop you from reaching Stage 2 and Stage 3.

This perspective on the primacy of the ego does not mean you can disregard the value of others or that you should battle others or compete with them for values. On the contrary, the primacy of the ego comes first as a principle that spurs action. Since this discovery of the ego is a thought process, it represents the ultimate reduction. It is a thinking process about the value of self, the value of "you" acting in reality". In this sense, the discovery of the centrality of the self is a normative process: the discovery of the "existence" of your self, as well as the "existence" of your value as a self (as an individual).

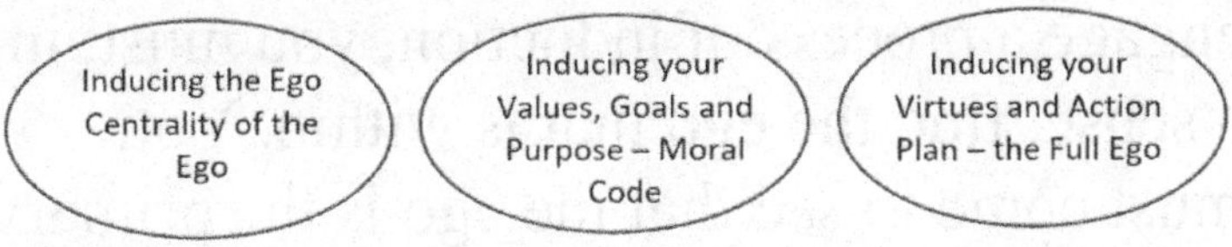

Stage 1 Stage 2 Stage 3

Notes:__________________________________

Stage 1. Centrality of the Ego

The first stage of studying the ego is to discover its nature and what it means to man to have an ego. The ego is not what you may think. It is not a source of evil, of bad actions, nor is it the cause of all your problems. To find your true ego, you must engage a process of induction, you must, in a sense, find the ego that is within. You must come to see that the ego is the primary concept that has meaning for your life. It is your driving force, in a sense.

Inducing the primacy of the ego requires an engagement, a study whose purpose is to learn where it resides. You must first look at human history to see the forces in history and how the ego was both involved and not involved in human living. You want to understand what makes the ego a central part of both the past and the present.

We start with observation. We find the ego as it exists in reality. We find examples of the ego and attempt to isolate the characteristics that make it what it is. At this point, the ego is an abstraction. It is not a thing in itself. It is a concept about which we are enquiring in order to understand its nature and its true role in human striving.

In a wonderful demonstration, Dr. Leonard Peikoff, in his lecture course, Objectivism Through Induction, makes a credible case for man's ability to induce egoism. The steps to induction, according to Dr. Peikoff include the following:

First, he starts by defining philosophy as "The study of fundamentals, and specifically of principles defining man's proper relationship to existence. I define philosophy as the science of man's relationship to existence. Metaphysics of course as a branch of philosophy brings in the fact of existence but every other branch is man's relation, how man should behave so as to conform to existence and thereby gain some crucial end. Epistemology defines the principles of proper thought so as to enable us to achieve cognition, knowledge. Ethics defines the principles of proper action so as to enable us to achieve survival. Government, the principles of proper social organization so as to enable us to protect individual rights. Art, the principles of the creation of art works so as to enable them to achieve their function of condensing philosophy. In all cases, it is a branch that studies how man should behave in a given area in order to conform to existence and thereby achieve a certain end. And the question is how would you ever know what principles reality requires for you to conform to it, and the only conceivable way is to discover them by the study of existence including the study of man, and therefore, the conclusion is that philosophic ideas have to be reached exclusively on the basis of observation of reality. They have to be learned and proved, read off from reality. And in this sense, philosophy is not unique, it is like any subject, whether you are studying beetles or stars or whatever. You have to start with observation. You do not properly, in any subject, start with books, people, or lectures. The only value of these things are for other people to report their observations to you and thereby save you time, or to guide you in making your own observations and save time, but the only cognitive source, the only source of actual knowledge is the study of the data out there. So, if you think of any subject at all, leaving aside introspection, the frame of reference is always outward. Your gaze when you are thinking, should be, your perspective, your focus, out there, outside. It should not be turned in on yourself. It should not be a process of memory when you are thinking. It should not be a process of trying to recall what was once clear to you. It is not digging in your subconscious for what was in some book or some lecture or what some person once said. Once you know a given fact and you file it in essentials, the relation between your mind and that fact, should be no longer mediated by other people in any way including by their books. You have to be literally the only man alive thinking of this subject. That's true of all subjects and its true equally of philosophy. A human source of your philosophy is a bad thing unless that's just a time saver that you drop out at a certain point. It should never be essential to you when you think of philosophy that I wrote a book or gave a lecture or that Ayn Rand wrote a book. That's fine, those things are fine as maps to point out where to look or to give you an advanced report on what she found. But you have to make the trip to be focused on the road and not on her report. So, the first message is when you're stuck, look out, do not look in. Don't try to take an inventory of the fragments that come to you from within your mind. Forget about that and look out.

"Now when we look out, we contact reality through perception of concretes. We have to reach the basic truths we are looking for, the principles by derivation from concretes. The name for that process of reaching principles from concretes is induction. And by the nature of philosophy, in fact of all science, that is the only way to proceed."

…

"Induction is generalization from concretes."[2]

Dr. Peikoff is speaking about inducing generalizations (principles) from concretes observed in existence. He is saying obtain your knowledge first hand by observing reality and drawing conclusions that you can validate by means of your own experience of reality and the knowledge you derive from it. This idea, this invocation of

---

[2] Objectivism Through Induction, lecture course by Dr. Leonard Peikoff, Lecture 1

observation as the means to knowledge can help you understand the foundation of human reason. This "looking outward" is the means for identifying the fact of human volition as the primary difference in man. As you look out, this is where you find the ego as the central force in life. This is where you will find the centrality of the ego in others and within yourself.

Dr. Peikoff attempts to induce other concepts before he gets to inducing egoism. He starts by inducing "cause and effect" as an example that would help us understand what induction is. His process of induction begins to take shape upon the foundation of existence, and we begin to understand that understanding is only possible on the foundation of "observation". As Dr. Peikoff declares early in this lecture, we must learn to "read off" of reality in order to learn the knowledge we need to develop our understanding of important concepts, especially the concept of the ego. He also stated that the words of others, their books, their lectures, etc. are merely guides to understanding, maps to the roads one can travel toward induction. Sometimes, theses guides are wrong and sometimes they are based on valid induction/science.

The best knowledge is based on observed reality, observed objects, and abstractions, facts derived from the process of induction.

The Process of Induction "Induction is a valid form of cognition without requiring any deductions to supplement it." – Peikoff
Explanatory Notes – Previously accepted Knowledge: Knowledge comes from sense experience. - Peikoff Sense experience comes from perception and observation. - Peikoff Reason is man's means of knowledge. – Ayn Rand A long process of induction leads to life as the standard. - Peikoff What is the foundational road to objective knowledge? It is volitional adherence to reality through the use of logic. – Aristotle To arrive at ethics, you learn that life is the standard. – Ayn Rand The law of identity is the means to discerning concrete reality. -Aristotle

The law cause and effect means that everything in reality acts according to its nature, even man. – Ayn Rand[3] "A thing of a certain kind acts in a certain way." - Peikoff	
Step 1	Define your terms/goals/or questions – induction of the primacy of the ego
Step 2	Define the rules of proof, observation of men acting in reality, pre-existing truths already verified (know your source).
Step 3	Find examples – a thing is what it is and acts according to its nature – find this by watching people act – why are they acting? Not by what they say or think, but what they do. What values do they seek?
Step 4	Generalization from examples. Reduce your general principle to "All S is P"
Step 5	Write your thesis – your statement of truth and the proof of it

[3] Requires the perceptual grasp of entities and/or concepts. "The law of causality is the law of identity applied to action. All actions are caused by entities." -Peikoff

Step 6	Create your maxims/fundamental principles/the rules you will live by. This is the “is/ought” expression of your chosen actions and values.

Notes:____

____

____

____

____

____

____

____

____

____

____

____

____

____

____

____

____

From Dr. Peikoff’s lecture:

“I want to tell you this point now. We did add something beyond generalization from instances. We did not add a deductive proof. What did we add by going through the law of identity and its tie into causality? We added a connection, an integration. We took a widespread observation, namely what led us to causality and tied it in to principles established by earlier observation. So, this is really the problem: We have an unlimited set of observations condensed into identity, and a distinct set of observations condensed into causality. Now most people, the best people today, see no connection between those two. They hear that the world is uniform and say, "Yeah, I can see that," and they hear that A is A and say, "Oh, yes, sure, I agree with that. I agree with logic," and they would never dream that there is a connection between those two. Now Aristotle saw the connection and Ayn Rand did. She saw what? That those two, identity and causality, fit together into one unit, that causality is an aspect of identity. I'll put it another way, all the concretes that come under causality also come under identity, along with lots of things that don't pertain to causality. This is a process of integration. Integration, by definition, is making a single whole out of parts. It is not the same as deduction. It is merely seeing that two things together make one."[4]

This policy of integration is the essence of the method you need in order to identify all other facts, objects, abstractions, and principles that connect your mind to reality in all respects. Induction is the method for integrating all aspects of your life.

More from Dr. Peikoff in this lecture:

"What it (integration) really does is reciprocally strengthen each element by combining them into a unit. That is the value of integration."

Let us review the steps of induction.

Step 1. Define your term/goal/or question – induction of the primacy of the ego. One way to understand the primacy of the ego is by contrasting it with its opposite which is altruism, the primacy of others. You can identify what altruism does to the individual who sacrifices his values and experiences loss and compare that loss to the individual who lives according to the primacy of the

[4] Ibid

ego which practice yields a positive gain of value (through production).

With altruism, the primacy of the ego is "given up" for the sake of the primacy of others. We do this by defining what the ego must be, what you expect to find and/or validate. You can look for the identity of the ego and the cause and effect of it which would be happiness, self-love, gain (not loss) and peace of mind. As Dr. Peikoff explains, you should want to experience this with your own mind, not by looking at what others think, but by looking at what you think when you look at reality, what you see and the generalizations you can derive from what you see. Reading a book like this one is not a bad thing as long as you use these books as road maps or guides to understanding reality. But essentially, your goal in this process of finding your ego is to use your mind to abstract from reality and understand with clarity what you are learning as you look outward.

Notes:______________________________________

____

____

____

____

____

____

____

____

____

____

____

____

____

____

____

____

____

____

____

____

____

Step 2. Define the rules of proof that will help you discover your ego, and its centrality in your life. Define the statements (general abstractions), the propositions that are an expression of the existence of the primacy of your ego. Look out to discover it out there, in the real world. Most people act with life as the standard of value (but many do not). Once you find the centrality of the ego, learn that people acting rationally always know how to act by identifying their values and then identifying the virtues that reflect life as the standard. Contemplate these virtues such as being rational (using induction and reason (being logical), practicing justice (by identifying the value or disvalue of others), being productive, honest, possessing integrity, contemplating the pride your virtues bring, as well as contemplating your self-esteem, seeing their reality in both expression and action. These discoveries require self-focus (focus on the self), ego-centrality, and focus on your self's growth and success.

You can also compare the results. Try to quantify the gains over time between sacrificing values (altruism) and gaining values (egoism). There is a difference in what you can gain from egoism and what you lose through altruism. These losses or gains are quantifiable and seeing them in tangible terms (how your life would be harmed with altruism and benefited with egoism) would be a valuable exercise.

Also consider the losses or gains that come in terms of the value to your spirit, or soul, in terms of the intangibles of love, happiness, and general peace of mind. It is egoism (life as the standard) that brings these, not giving up as the standard. You can also learn to contemplate the value of being an objective thinker and compare that to the disvalue that comes from mysticism and rationalism (that depart from reality and require bold leaps into false knowledge). Anti-egoism and anti-mind views lead over time to nihilism and they destroy your ability to know the values that a thinking mind can help you create.

Notes:______________________________

Step 3. "A thing is what it is and acts according to its nature" – find this general principle by watching people act – Answer questions such as "when thinking about accomplishing a specific value, "what is the value, who is the beneficiary, and what is the ultimate goal?"

In order to identify the existence of the ego, you must first identify the existence of the human mind and how it functions, what are the purposes to which the mind is dedicated, or should be dedicated. Look for examples of the proper uses of the human mind in the actions and expressions of other individuals. Look at both good and bad individuals and try to identify how they use their minds to create both good and bad in life.

Additionally, look around you and try to connect the actions and expressions of others to how they use virtue (of the lack thereof) to create outcomes (good and bad) in their lives. Try to find examples of the primacy of the ego in the actions and thoughts of others. Look for examples of rational thinking, productiveness, independence (both intellectual and financial), integrity, justice, pride, self-respect, accomplishment, love, self-value, self-esteem, etc. Find examples of how people validate their own egos to help you conclude that the ego is a thing that exists in reality, and that it is ubiquitous or universal. Find enough examples of egoism so your observation convinces you that egoism, the primacy of the ego, is either good or bad. Use your own mind here, not the minds of moralists or moral dictators, use your own observations and keep doing this until you can draw general principles from your observations. This may take some time but don't give up.

Notes:______________________________

Step 4. Reduce your general principle to "All S is P". Determine when you have clearly found the "All" in "All S is P" such as "all ego-primacy is good".

Notes:

Step 5. Develop your thesis after you have collected all of your facts. Take Step 4 and your examples and illustrate, or demonstrate your truth that All S is P. “All egoism is life as the standard”, for instance.

Notes:______________________________

Step 6. Define what your thesis means in terms of human action, what you should do once this knowledge is in place in your mind and life. We talk here about "is/ought" principles. If the ego is primary with you, what ought you do to accomplish the life of achievement you seek and the happiness/self-esteem that will be the result.

Notes:____

If the individual holds his ego as his ultimate, primary value, he establishes the foundation and justification for putting together all of the facts that will help him create his moral code. This moral code sets the stage for the full ego (or gets as close as possible to it). This is the most powerful way for an individual to learn about and establish his moral abilities: by learning that his ego stands ahead of any other consideration of moral premises.

This premise of the centrality of the ego stands opposed to any moral injunction (or imperative) that requires that the individual submit to the moral views of others, or to any subcategories of morality that he holds. It is the isolation of the ego, as an end in itself, that enables the development of full morality. In fact, this premise of the primacy of the ego is the foundation for an understanding of how EGOnomics works to protect the individual from religious and modern philosophy's assaults on the ego and the mind. In fact, full morality, egoism, and the primacy of the ego, preclude submission in any way to the minds of others.

Defining your moral code requires the same (or a similar) process that was used to validate the centrality of the ego. In this stage you validate the moral code you will use when it comes to practicing or effecting your moral code in action.

The Process of Induction "Induction is a valid form of cognition without requiring any deductions to supplement it." – Peikoff
Explanatory Notes – Previously accepted Knowledge: Knowledge comes from sense experience. - Peikoff Sense experience comes from perception. - Peikoff Reason is man's means of knowledge – Ayn Rand A long process of induction leads to life as the standard. - Peikoff What is objective knowledge? It is volitional adherence to reality through the use of logic. – Aristotle Life is the standard – Ayn Rand The law of identity – Aristotle

The law cause and effect – Ayn Rand[5] "A thing of a certain kind acts in a certain way." - Peikoff	
Step 1	Define your terms/goals/or questions – induction of the values you will pursue – engage this process for each of the major values which are reason, purpose, self-esteem.
Step 2	Define the rules of proof, pre-existing truths already verified (know your source),
Step 3	Find examples of values and the consequences of values to the lives of other people and yourself – a thing is what it is and acts according to its nature – find this by watching people act – why are they acting? What values do they seek? What is their reason for pursuing these values? How do they validate their values? By dealing with the reality of their values.

[5] Requires the perceptual grasp of entities and/or concepts. "The law of causality is the law of identity applied to action. All actions are caused by entities." -Peikoff

Step 4	Generalization from examples. Reduce your general principle to "All S is P"
Step 5	Write your thesis – your statement of your values and the proof of each of them – make a list in hierarchical order. Some values achieve life as a standard better than others.

What will all this look like? How will it lead to your full ego? When you define your moral principles, at each step, you will have validated your ego and the centrality of your ego as the primary motive and basis of your moral code. This will lay the moral foundation for life as the standard and, finally, it will give you the means, reason and reality, to practice (act) with your full ego at all times. The more correct actions you take and, as you realize the success you accomplish, you will begin to feel the ultimate pride and self-esteem that come from your moral knowledge.

Step 1 Define your terms/goals/or questions – induction of the values you will pursue – engage this process for each of the major values which are reason, purpose, self-esteem.

Notes:______________________________

Step 2 Define the rules of proof, pre-existing truths already verified (know your source)

Notes:______________________________

Step 3 Find examples of values and the consequences of values to the lives of other people and yourself – a thing is what it is and acts according to its nature – find this by watching people act – why are they acting? What values do they seek? What is their reason for pursuing these values? How do they validate their values? By dealing with the reality of their values.

Notes:

Step 4 Generalization from examples. Reduce your general principle to “All S is P”.

Notes:

Step 5 Write your thesis – your statement of your values and the proof of each of them – make a list in hierarchical order. Some values achieve life as a standard better than others.

Notes:

Stage 3. Creating the Full Ego

Discovering the full ego requires the art of defining your values, your goals, and your purpose. It also requires rating them within a specific context, comparing them so you eventually arrive at the point of knowing the central core that animates your purpose in life. The upshot is that, morally, putting the self in a central position requires thinking, integrity, evaluation, logic, and the desire to be highly moral.

The Process of Induction "Induction is a valid form of cognition without requiring any deductions to supplement it." – Peikoff
Explanatory Notes – Previously accepted Knowledge: Knowledge comes from sense experience. - Peikoff Sense experience comes from perception. - Peikoff Reason is man's means of knowledge – Ayn Rand A long process of induction leads to life as the standard. - Peikoff

What is objective knowledge? It is volitional adherence to reality through the use of logic. – Aristotle Life is the standard – Ayn Rand The law of identity -Aristotle The law cause and effect – Ayn Rand[6] “A thing of a certain kind acts in a certain way.” - Peikoff	
Step 1	Define your terms/goals/or questions – induction of the virtues you will practice to achieve your values – engage this process for each of the major virtues, rationality, productiveness, pride, honesty, integrity, independence, justice.
Step 2	Define the rules of proof, pre-existing truths already verified (know your source).
Step 3	Find examples – a thing is what it is and acts according to its nature – find this by watching people act – why are they acting? What values do they seek? Of value to whom (beneficiary), for what (for what

[6] Requires the perceptual grasp of entities and/or concepts. “The law of causality is the law of identity applied to action. All actions are caused by entities.” -Peikoff

	goal), and how (the practice of reason).
Step 4	Generalization from examples. Reduce your general principle to "All S is P".
Step 5	Write your virtues down – your statement of the virtues you will practice, and the proof of each of them as well as the specific acts you will take to accomplish your purpose in life.

Step 1. Define your terms/goals/or questions – induction of the virtues you will practice to achieve your values – engage this process for each of the major virtues, rationality, productiveness, pride, honesty, integrity, independence, justice. If you have found other virtues, define them as well.

Notes:____

Step 2. Define the rules of proof, pre-existing truths already verified (know your source).

Notes:

Step 3. Find examples – a thing is what it is and acts according to its nature – find this by watching people act – why are they acting? What values do they seek? Of value to whom (beneficiary), for what (for what goal), and how (the practice of reason).

Notes:____

Step 4. Generalization from examples. Reduce your general principle to "All S is P". "This virtue is this recognition of reality."

Notes:____

Step 5. Write your virtues down – your statement of the virtues you will practice, and the proof of each of them as well as the specific acts you will take to accomplish your purpose in life.

Notes:

Properly, the individual belongs to himself, and he should resist ideas that declare a collective obligation to live for others. I adhere to the idea that an individual should strive for his "full ego", he should live according to the tenets of egoism and individualism and take the steps that will accomplish life as the standard. As we will see, it is possible to divide egoism into full egoism, mixed egoism, and narcissism.

If the full ego exists as a practical concept, men can also conclude that all other things, objects, concepts (abstractions), values, virtues, and facts, are real, and since they are derived from the mind looking at reality, the ego is free to live according to correct moral knowledge. There can be nothing "mixed" about moral knowledge. Either knowledge is true, or it is not knowledge.

Notes:

Calculating your Full Ego

There is no tried-and-true way to calculate how close you are getting toward your full ego. I would like to suggest the following approach:

We will use two elements. First, we will look at your chosen list of values. For example, let us say your following values include first your cardinal values: Reason, Purpose, and Self-Esteem. Let us assume that you found yourself engaged in five acts of reason, two acts toward your purpose, and one act of notable self-esteem. Keep in mind that the goal with each act is a clearly known value based upon life as the standard.

Cardinal Values		
Reason	Purpose	Self-Esteem
✓✓✓✓✓	✓✓	✓
Description		
4 acts at work – notable	1 act attended	1 scored goal in

improvements of product	college classes 1 act proposed to Helen – she said "yes"	soccer game
Value List		
Write 1st book – 25 pages – 1 check	Learned new recipe – it tasted great – 1 check	Read Aristotle – 1 chapter – 1 check
✓✓	✓	✓✓
Make 25 extra sales	Call parents	Learn speed reading
✓✓	✓	✓
To Do List		
Learn sales techniques	Read how to do the big sale	Read for fun
✓	X	X

Run every other day	Exercise at gym	Get up early
X	✓	X
Listen to logic lecture	Study history of philosophy	Watch a movie with Helen
✓✓	X	✓
Negatives		
Argued with my brother	Cursed	Looked at a pretty lady in front of Helen
X	✓ (Didn't Curse)	X
Positives		
Had great meeting with boss	Earned praise for an article I wrote	Told only clean jokes

X	✓	✓

Needless to say, this is an example. To calculate your percent of effectiveness toward your full ego, count up all ✓s and Xs.

A	Total ✓s and Xs	33
B	Total ✓s	24
C	Percent (divide B by A) (B/A=%)	72%

You are at 72 % of your full ego.

Here is a blank sheet to use:

Cardinal Values		
Reason	Purpose	Self-Esteem
Description		
Value List		

To Do List		
Negatives		
Positives		

To calculate your percent of effectiveness toward your full ego, count up all ✓s and Xs (A), count up all ✓s (B) and divide B by A. (B / A = percent of your full ego you have achieved.

A	Total ✓s and Xs	
B	Total ✓s	
C	Percent (divide B by A) (B/A=%)	

End of newly copyrighted material from 2023.

Step 6. Feel your Values

But this is more than just a list. If there is anything to feel passionate about (or to love), it can only be something that you have validated as in your best interest. There is nothing wrong with it (in fact, it is very good) loving your values so much that you only think about how to pursue and achieve them.

You should learn to cherish your values because of their importance in your life. Learn to *feel* them and how much they mean to you, especially those values that are fundamental to your life, your mind, your needs and those people you love. They are not just lines of text on a piece of paper, they are the reason you live.

It can help you tremendously to learn just how deeply you love them and how much they mean to you especially when you compare them to the artificial and poorly chosen disvalues that might be harming your life. See your true values in perspective and put your disvalues in their proper place as unimportant things you really don't value at all.

Now go through each value you have written down above and ask yourself how strongly you feel about this value. How much does it mean to you? Be as expressive and deep as possible and especially compare it to its negative counterpart from Step 4.

Which has a more powerful attraction to you and why?

Notes:

The critical point for you always comes at the time when your feelings and your reason conflict. Your troublesome emotions are based upon your past faulty thinking; they give you rationalizations and they drive your body to do what you subconsciously want to do. This is the decision point where you need to confront your bad emotions, question them and defeat them for their irrationality. This will help you create a new decision point that is based upon your self-interest and values.

The better you get this thought process out into the open, the better for you. The more you engage in the process, the closer you will get to understanding what is going on inside your mind and the better you will be at controlling it and making the right decisions.

Some tips:

1. If you fail, it isn't the end of the world. You just have to try to do better next time. Mentally record what you thought in that moment of decision and especially make sure you record how strongly your subconscious fought to make you do it. This will serve you well when that moment of decision comes again. You will know what to expect. The more mental notes you write down, the

stronger will be your ability to prepare for what to expect at important moments of decision.

Notes:____

2. As we have discussed above, you need independence of thought. It is easy to fall back into thinking the way other people think. We've been taught to do that all our lives. But it is critical on this point

that you think independently and avoid, as much as possible, following old ways of thinking. It is your life; not the life of other people. It is your mind and you must pave your own path if you are going to understand yourself.

Notes:_______________________________________

3. The key point is that moment of decision. It is there where the inner-deception takes place. It at this moment where you can catch yourself. Ask yourself to be more specific about your reason for choosing the activity. For instance, "Why do you think you need to eat right now?" "Who are you trying to please in consenting to this activity?" Be as precise as you can and try to dig deep into what is going on in your mind. Make it explicit so you can check the facts and argue against it.

Notes:______________________________________

____

____

____

____

____

____

____

____

____

____

____

____

____

____

____

Step 7. Learn to See Reality

The key with this step is to know the difference between true knowledge (realism) and false knowledge (rationalization). Once you acquire this ability, you can then begin to base your actions on truth rather than falsehood.

I've written elsewhere that reason is "cognitive" in nature. When I say "cognitive", I mean that human thinking has the goal of understanding reality as it is. In other words, when you say, "I see a table" you mean that you actually see the object that is defined as a "four-legged object with a flat surface". Apply this principle to your entire range of experience and you will understand that you can see reality as it is and that your mind has the tools that enable you to make correct decisions.

You might have been taught that the mind is incapable of judging and knowing reality but this view is part of the problem. How can you know that this is true by means of your mind?

At some point, you'll have to take a stand regarding the issue of what is real and what is not. Eventually, you must then move from what is real to what is morally proper. The second should be based upon the first. As we argued in the book, The REAL Purpose-Driven Life, every is implies an ought. Without the "is", you will never arrive at the ought or else you'll be perennially tied to uncertainty.

I learned that establishing firm knowledge today is very difficult because both religion and modern philosophy are bent on ensuring that you are confused about the nature of what is real. Yet, that knowledge is what you need in order to understand the world and how your problems fit in.

So, what should you do? Challenge your family, your teachers, your professors and everyone you have known in your life? That may not always be the "proper" thing to do because some of them will be offended that you disagree with them. Some of them tell you they are certain there is no such thing as certainty.

Yet, your mind *is* capable of understanding reality. There are certain truths that hold and it is possible for you to discover those truths. Existence exists and it is the job of your mind to understand it.[7] In the future, use this section to write about some of the conflicts you have with people and with yourself over the issue of what is real and what is not.

---

[7] I am not the first person to say this. Ayn Rand developed an entire philosophy of life around these propositions.

Notes:

Extra chapter: Step 8. Moving from Values to Purpose

How does one define one's purpose? This is a complex issue and depends heavily on your ability to self-evaluate and introspect. Here are some suggestions. Use the open lines to write your thoughts down:

The first guide is to ensure that your values are defined by you with your own mind, not by the others in your life. The process of doing this involves a conscious process of identifying how to develop your own knowledge. Today, any individual who cares for his own life must educate himself; must seek out knowledge about logic, the development of normative values and how to engage in the process of inductive reasoning. If you are not actively pursuing this knowledge, I suggest that, for the sake of living a moral life, it is time to begin the quest.

Notes:____________________________________

____

____

____

____

____

Secondly, ensure that your purpose is based upon your deepest values, those things that you want to bring into the world as expressions of your individual soul. For many people, defining this is difficult because they are so influenced by the opinions and values of others. An unfortunately large number of people spend many years pursuing values they have not validated according to a standard of their own. Once again, our schools barely touch on this issue and, most often, many young people are manipulated into accepting values that involve self-sacrifice and do not reflect the real needs and qualities of the individual, his happiness or wellbeing.

Notes:

Thirdly, ensure that your purpose is achievable in the long-term and that you know how you will achieve it through your actions, your personal schedule, and your abilities. If you need to earn a certain educational level in order to fulfil your purpose, you should plan to go to college. If you need to be in superlative physical condition, make sure you know what is required and how you will accomplish it. In essence, you need to plan all of the activities that will put you in the proper position to achieve your purpose. The benefit of this approach is that you will know exactly what you will need to do to be successful and you will know that not pursuing these pre-purpose activities will make it harder for you to accomplish it.

Notes: ______________________________

Your values were most likely developed over the course of your life. Your purpose was not likely something that your parents or teachers discussed. This is why it is important for you to identify your values; they can give you a clue about what your purpose should be.

When I say "purpose", I'm not talking about a "programmed" goal that you pursue robotically. I'm talking about something you choose and commit your life to accomplishing. It is something supremely important to YOU.

The key fact about purpose is that it integrates your life. You build your life around the values that make up your purpose. The expression of your purpose is an expression of your values and guides your actions toward their accomplishment.

To determine your purpose, you need to decide what you want in life. Take a look at your values list and ask yourself which category of values is the most important to you personally. Which of these value sets represents not only your professional life but also the values that you love most; the values that you would enjoy pursuing and advancing. This should give you your purpose in life. Write down below what you have decided is your purpose and why:

Notes:______________________________________

____

____

____

____

____

____

____

____

____

____

____

____

____

____

____

____

____

____

Now that you have defined your purpose, you will want to look at these values again and decide which will need to be adjusted or which new values you should add to the category that you hadn't thought of. Perhaps you need more education to pursue this value effectively or you may need to spend more time in working, studying or traveling.

Once you have done this, you'll want to create a "subcategory" for each major value which is a step toward it. Here, you will want to develop an overall strategy that takes you step-by-step to preparing for your purpose and developing a comprehensive strategy for its pursuit.

Congratulations, you now know your purpose in life and what you must do to accomplish it. Now you have a much better sense of who you are and a stronger motive for working toward your values. Now go back to your Cardinal values and you'll notice how important they are to the accomplishment of your purpose. In particular, look at the Cardinal value of self-esteem.

Self-esteem should now be even more important than you might have thought before. You have to have a conviction that you are worth it, that you are good; and you must work to understand what your self is and learn to appreciate your unique soul and spirit.

To get self-esteem you must develop your self, learn about your self, grow as a person. Self-esteem makes it possible to understand your purpose. Learning who you are and appreciating it can be a powerful motivating factor for you but you must be the center of it, not someone else.

Self-esteem and the other three cardinal values are part of your makeup, part of what you need and must seek if you are to have a fulfilling life. You need your self and you must pursue it relentlessly. Write something below about what you have learned about the importance for your life of reason, purpose and self-esteem. Think it through thoroughly like we thought through existence and positivity before:

Notes:______________________________

We are writing here about absolute selfishness and it is based on the absolute necessity of pursuing reason, purpose and self-esteem; the absolute necessity of these concepts for your life and your ability to survive. Selfishness is, indeed, a virtue because it means living according to your own mind, for your own goals and with your own happiness as the result. Consider the alternatives.

To pursue your purpose, you must make an effort to adhere to reality, to take an inductive approach to life where facts determine what you will accept as truth and where you understand that your self-esteem and purpose are yours to create by means of your focus on facts, on reality and on the requirements of reality.

Life requires selfishness, effort and action and because so, the more selfish you are, the better your focus on learning how to think (reason) and how to create your own value (self-esteem) and purpose in life (morality), the more successful and happy you will be.

Let's look at the alternative. If you are taught that reason is not important, that it is weak and ineffective, you will not learn how to use your mind. You will think that all you need is to listen to your parents, peers, preachers, God, etc. and this will guide you away from your own interests. You will think that no man is an island and take your views from the generally accepted ideas you find around you.

There is no certainty in this approach. If you consider your purpose in life to be sacrifice to others, you will not apply yourself to a purpose you will love; you will do only what is necessary to appease social and cultural authorities. You will not consider what will actually make you happy; you will not find a purpose that suits you. You will only find a purpose that suits others.

Notes:______________________________

If self-esteem is not a value for you, you will think that others are more important than you. You will become a Babbitt, a softie, a person who has no real convictions, no real self and you will not even know the basis upon which to found your happiness and self-respect. If you think this person sounds familiar, it is the common man of today; hopefully it is not you.

The attacks made upon man's ego, such as they are, are essentially attacks on the pursuit of these three values (Reason, Purpose, Self-Esteem). The intent of these attacks is to destroy your ability to live, to act and to think. These three top values require work, planning, struggle, sometimes innovative thinking and lots of time working on yourself.

Notes:

Reason means looking at the world, drawing generalizations, understanding causality and recognizing that the world is a place where you can be successful; reason is nothing more than good thinking; but it is good thinking that operates according to the nature of reality; because the purpose of your consciousness is to use knowledge to make decisions about what you will do and why.

Notes:

With a foundation of practiced virtues, you can support your purpose; what you want to create in the world by means of your virtues, the goals you want to work toward. This could include a career, love, leisure, work but they must be *your* values identified by you and they must be consistent with reason, purpose and self-esteem – nothing is more important than reason (your clear thinking), purpose (your goals in life) and your love of your self. You have to work for all this.

In order to be happy, you must know what you value and why. You must be able to look at reality and decide what is good for you and how you will accomplish it. You must know what your key values will bring to your life and you must understand the purpose that these values bring about.

Notes:______________________________________

____

____

____

____

____

____

____

____

____

____

____

____

____

____

____

____

____

____

I hope you have enjoyed this book and that it has given you many good ideas on how to become a happy person living life according to your highest aspirations. If you have any questions, don't hesitate to contact me by email at robertv1989@outlook.com.

About Robert Villegas

Robert Villegas is an American writer born in Weslaco, TX. He is an independent philosopher with a strong focus on the practical consequences of ideas. He considers the philosophy of ideas to be a central factor in creating a better society and he offers both a critical discussion of modern philosophy as well as practical solutions and fundamental principles to solve problems associated with pragmatism and indeterminacy. His work stands on its own.

Mr. Villegas spent over twenty-seven years as a UPS executive in Indiana and worked in locations all over Europe such as Germany, England, and Spain. At UPS he worked as a Call Center Manager and Telecommunications Manager. He was involved in helping to transition UPS from paper-based processes to computerized networks and digital record keeping. He worked with early digital technologies and was one of the first telecommunications managers to develop a system for communicating to drivers while they were on their routes.

After leaving UPS, Mr. Villegas started his own sport marketing company specializing in writing sponsorship proposals for race car drivers and other athletes. Clients included Johnny Parsons, Jeff Ward, Larry Foyt and Alexander Rossi to name a few. He also worked as a technical writer in the burgeoning telecommunications industry in South Florida where he created many successful sales presentations and marketing documents. He also built his company's first website and worked for companies throughout the country including New York City, Boston, San Francisco, Sacramento, Chicago, Miami, Minneapolis, Vancouver BC, and other locations.

In 2015, he began to pursue his life-long goal of becoming a published author and has written about 109 books to date in areas such as novels, theater, religion, poetry, philosophy, and business. During this period, he also wrote over 260 Business

Plans mostly for companies in Canada. He also wrote grant proposals and developed grant proposal narratives for several organizations, earning millions of dollars for fire departments and charitable organizations.

He has also served in the US Military as a communications specialist and served his tour of duty during the Vietnam era in Korea near the DMZ. He was raised in Indiana and presently lives in Arizona.

He was educated in Indiana and earned a Degree through the University of the State of NY (Albany) via an external degree program when he came out of the military. He is divorced with three grown children and three grandchildren. Famous relatives include Mexican anti-hero Dimas DeLeon and guitarist and music producer Johnny Garcia of Weslaco, TX.

Alcoholism and Addiction – the System

These four books comprise a system that can be used by both patients and counselors who are battling Alcoholism and Addiction. Based upon Mr. Villegas's own system developed during his struggle against alcoholism, this system includes:

Alcoholism and Addiction – A Secular Ten-Step Program

This groundbreaking book offers a secular approach to alcoholism unlike that offered by Alcoholics Anonymous. We recommend that every individual going for alcohol and drug-abuse counseling be given a copy of this book which contains the workbook and the two versions of The World's first drunk. http://amzn.to/2md6R9w $3.45 Kindle $11.95 softcover

The Secular Ten-Step Program Workbook

This booklet covers the program developed by Mr. Villegas. It is designed as a workbook with blank spaces for the patient to write his own thoughts as he takes each of the ten steps. Order one copy for each patient in counseling. http://amzn.to/2lrHimS $4.49 Kindle $6.95 softcover

The World's First Drunk – With Counselor Talking Points

This booklet is designed for the counselor as he works with patients during individual or group therapy. It contains helpful tips on discussing the life story of the man who invented alcohol. Order one copy for each patient in counseling. http://amzn.to/2l446Wr $2.99 Kindle $5.95 softcover

The World's First Drunk – Patient Version

This version of the short story contains empty spaces where the patient can answer questions about the life story of the man who invented alcohol. Order one copy for each counselor. http://amzn.to/2ldxBGb $2.99 Kindle $5.95 softcover.

Business Books by Robert Villegas

These four books by Robert Villegas comprise some of the business books that he has written. As an executive working for several companies, he was able to develop these methods that will help anyone seeking to excel in the business world. These books are:

How to Be a Great Employee – and a Greater Manager

You cannot be a great manager without first being a great employee. And this is something that requires learning, experience and attitude. The attitude comes from you but the learning and experience you should acquire through diligent study and practice. http://amzn.to/2BqdG2i $3.99 Kindle $8.95 softcover

SWOT Analysis Supercharged

A SWOT Analysis is an objective look at the internal and external elements of your organization that impact your success or lack thereof. If done diligently, you will always have a handle on what you need to do to improve season after season. http://amzn.to/2BCAWYx $3.99 Kindle $6.95 softcover

The Five-Module Call Center Training System

The Five-Module Call Center Training System is designed to assist the Call Center Team Leader in helping his employees quickly upgrade their skills to an acceptable level. http://amzn.to/2B3Svj1 $3.99 Kindle $5.95 softcover

Website Development Methodology

Effective strategic marketing requires the ability to differentiate the website development organization and its deliverables from those of the competition. http://amzn.to/2DnYMqh $2.99 Kindle $12.95 softcover.

Books on Religion

The
Mark
of Titus

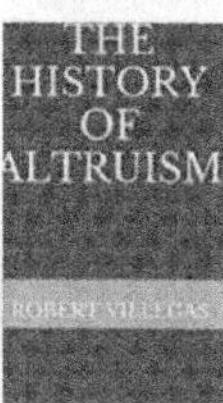

The Mark of Titus
Excerpts from the book Unkilling Jesus which highlight some of the key discoveries implied by new theories about the origin of the Jesus Myth. The idea that the Romans invented Christianity is the basic premise of new theories about the origin of Christianity .http://amzn.to/2itMCo0 $3.49 Kindle $5.95 softcover

Contra Religion
This book is designed as a "shorter" explanation of the ideas presented in my larger book, "Behind the Ritual Mask" which seeks to define fundamental principles of religion. I'm hoping this book will serve as a primer for the original book and spur an interest in reading it. http://amzn.to/2yWMSlx $3.99 Kindle $6.95 softcover

Is this the Face that Launched a Thousand Ships?
It was love at first sight. I saw her one day while watching a television program about King Tut, whose tomb had been discovered by Howard Carter years before. I was looking at the famous bust of a beautiful Egyptian Queen. https://amzn.to/3t487x3 $3.99 Kindle $7.95 softcover

The History of Altruism
The History of Altruism is a historical treatment of the development of altruism throughout time from the Paleolithic period to today. It tracks the development of self-sacrifice of primitive man to the advent of altruism as a development from Kant's "duty". It covers a broad sweep of concepts and shows how they influenced modern man, religion and societies through the ages. https://amzn.to/3gN8zgy $4.19 Kindle 14.95 paperback.

Books on Christianity

Unkilling Jesus
Who was Paul and what was his role in the creation of Christianity? What was his provenance, and did he meet the resurrected Christ? Who wrote Revelation and what was the document's purpose? Why was Domitian assassinated?
http://amzn.to/2itMCo0 $3.99 Kindle $15.95 softcover

Domitian: The Final Messiah
The central goal of this book is to define the specific themes and concepts that make up Domitian's contribution to Christianity – in a sense, we are defining the specific Domitian overlay to the Christian materials originally developed for Titus.
http://amzn.to/2yWMSlx $2.99 Kindle $6.95 softcover

Paul's Agon and the Mystification of History
Paul and Jesus are joined in one important way; the way of a miracle. They met on the road to Damascus while Paul supposedly pursued Christians. Jesus, in a sense, told Paul to get with the program and stop persecuting his people. In this incident, the Bible tells us that Jesus is already dead, and resurrected. This book argues otherwise.
http://amzn.to/2zSDsuP $5.99 Kindle $19.95 softcover

Christianity on the Arch of Titus
This book explores the "persons" visible on the Triumphant Arch of Titus which is located in the heart of Rome. These people were significant in that they played a role, not only in Rome's conquest of Judaea but also in the creation of Christianity. This book explores those individuals and the roles they played in the creation of one of the most important religious movements in world history.
https://amzn.to/3xz3OgM $3.69 Kindle 10.95 paperback.

The REAL Purpose-Driven Life

The REAL Purpose-Driven Life
After centuries of being told that it is not about you, it is time to set the record straight. You are a unique individual and your goal in life should be to achieve your own happiness.
https://amzn.to/2XyrpPf $3.50 Kindle $7.95 softcover

Values and Purpose Workbook
This book is about you. It's about time. After centuries of being told that nothing is about you, it is time to set the record straight. You are a unique individual and your goal in life should be to achieve your happiness. https://amzn.to/2XwlkTv $3.99 Kindle $8.95 softcover

Values and Purpose Books by Robert Villegas

The Real Purpose-Driven Life
After centuries of being told that it is not about you, it is time to set the record straight. You are a unique individual and your goal in life should be to achieve your own happiness. This book is about helping you accomplish your goals and fixing your purpose firmly in place. It covers not only why you should pursue your goals but how to do it.
https://amzn.to/3ebkhjr $3.99 Kindle $6.95 softcover

The Values and Purpose Workbook
Rather than give you tasks that involve doing a lot of things for other people, I'm am going to tell you that focusing on yourself will reveal your life's purpose and express your passions and freedom. I'm going to start with you.
https://amzn.to/3eQf4wG $2.99 Kindle $6.95 softcover

This Book is About You
Some people move briskly bent on a purpose, concerned only about what they are about. Some people walk by them; and do not even notice. They just keep to their path. This book is about you. It's about time. https://amzn.to/3vFMzss
$2.99 Kindle $5.95 softcover

Revelation

These three books are based upon a new perspective on the document named Revelation. Based upon a new theory of the story of Jesus as an invention of the Roman Imperial Cult, these books add significant new evidence for this theory.

Coded Messages in the Pastorals

The first book in the series on Revelation. I see Christianity, as we know it today, as an outgrowth of mostly one mind and one perspective and that is the mind and perspective of Paul the apostle who was the alter-ego for another man who lived and wrote in the AD 80s and AD 90s. https://amzn.to/3xx2Gdm $4.69 Kindle $10.95 softcover

The Seven Letters of Revelation

The second book on the three-book series on Revelation. The idea that Domitian was the author, through John, of Revelation is a relatively new idea. But, if this is true, it answers many questions about the purpose of Revelation and what events led up to it. By connecting the document to Domitian, we are also able to connect it to Pauline Christianity and understand the context for both Christian writings and Revelation. https://amzn.to/3aLekb4 $3.99 Kindle $6.95 softcover

Understanding the Book of Revelation

The third in the three-book series on Revelation, Understanding the Book of Revelation is the third and final book in the series about the conflict between Paul and Domitian over Paul's version of Christianity which is found in the gospels. https://amzn.to/3tWn6dH $5.19 Kindle $8.95 softcover

Self-Help Books by Robert Villegas

Existence a Rational Thoughtbook

A Rational Thoughtbook is designed for thinking as opposed to reading. It combines brief prescient content with stunning imagery. Existence focuses on the nature of existence and gives you intelligent thoughts to integrate into your life.
https://amzn.to/2RZpsKV $4.99 Kindle $12.95 softcover

The Virtue of Independence

One of the most important goals for any person is to establish intellectual independence. Intellectual independence is the road to "life" independence, which is the ability to earn your own way without help from others. https://amzn.to/3awuCV2 $2.99 Kindle $6.95 softcover

Rational Meditation

Rational Meditation is self-meditation. It is thinking about yourself without guilt and without the tenets of modern philosophy (that the world is unknowable, that man is a phony, that ethics and living are only about others). https://amzn.to/3gus9OE $6.99 Kindle $12.95 softcover

History of My Mind

This booklet is the companion to my book entitled Rational Meditation. It utilizes the various exercises of the original book that involve contemplation or meditation and provide space for written input by the reader. https://amzn.to/3gy3hpl $4.69 Kindle $11.95 softcover.

Rational Thoughtbooks by Robert Villegas

Existence a Rational Thoughtbook

A Rational Thoughtbook is designed for thinking as opposed to reading. It combines brief prescient content with stunning imagery. Existence focuses on the nature of existence and gives you intelligent thoughts to integrate into your life. https://amzn.to/2RZpsKV $4.99 Kindle $12.95 softcover

Identity

One of the most important goals for any person is to establish intellectual independence. Intellectual independence is the road to "life" independence, which is the ability to earn your own way without help from others. https://amzn.to/3nf9aJn $3.99 Kindle $9.95 softcover

Fiction and Creative Poems and Plays

Poetic Prose and Poetry
These expressions represent some of Mr. Villegas' deepest thoughts as he lived and traveled throughout the world in locations such as Germany (East and West), Austria, Britain, Spain, Canada, France, Luxembourg, Belgium, the Netherlands, Korea, New York, Miami, San Francisco and other locations. https://amzn.to/3vu7X3B $2.99 Kindle $6.95 softcover

The Lost Poems
These poems were discovered among Mr. Villegas's archives in 2016. Many of them have been read by only Mr. Villegas. Most of these poems were rejected as "not that good". After seeing them again, he has changed his mind. These poems expressive, fresh and spontaneously honest. https://amzn.to/3aPg5nB $3.99 Kindle $6.95 softcover

Adam Reborn – A Short Play
Adam Reborn is a play of symbols. Adam and Eve, as I have portrayed them, are young and heroic people learning to deal with a Paradise and God that are hostile to them. There is no chance of life for them. https://amzn.to/3u9Nr8b $2.99 Kindle $6.95 softcover

The Boy Who Stood Alone
Jonny Payne has just discovered Ayn Rand and his parents don't know what to do. They take him to a priest and a psychologist but his only question is "What is the price of independence? https://amzn.to/3nCG6ve $3.99 Kindle $6.95 paperback.

Fiction and Creative Materials

Aphrodite

Johnny is a Spanish guitar player with a mysterious past. At a party, he meets the beautiful songstress Aphrodite who is enthralled with his flamenco guitar skills. Later, she learns they have a connection, a particular song they both appear to know. Aphrodite discovers the connection, and through dreams, the two fall in love. The question is whether they will ever be together. https://amzn.to/3xIlmXZ $3.99 Kindle $5.95 softcover

The Odyssey of Amerigo the Founder

Amerigo was born in a time of desperation and dystopia. He was the only man with the vision of a great future. Many repaired to his cause while others swore to destroy him. They wanted his life, his mind and everything he loved. He swore that no matter what they did, he would win the struggle for freedom and a new future. https://amzn.to/2Qz8h2t $3.99 Kindle $8.95 softcover

Bob and Bobbie

1967 - a town outside Camp Casey, Korea - two young people have come together to challenge a world that makes love impossible. https://amzn.to/3sZWSpf $2.99 Kindle $5.95 softcover

The Raven Haired Girl

Bobby met Angie 52 years ago in a poor neighborhood in Indianapolis. It was love at first sight. For a few short months, their relationship blossomed into love. They were in love but didn't know how to be in love because they were only fourteen years old. https://amzn.to/3306plF $2.99 Kindle $6.95 paperback.

Other Books by Robert Villegas

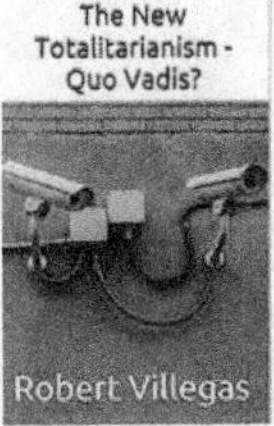

Naming Names in the NT

"Discovery consists of seeing what everybody has seen and thinking what nobody has thought." - Albert Szent-Gyogyi – 1937 Nobel Laureate
https://amzn.to/3mXR66H **$3.99 Kindle $9.95 softcover $16.95 hardcover**

Finding Your Soft Cry

Every individual has a yearning to know that he is both free and good. This yearning comes to him from early youth, and he hopes that he eventually develops the intellectual tools to help him distinguish between his nature and the demands of society. The key to freedom is the ability to act without restriction and, especially, without guilt. https://amzn.to/3p8lY7m **$3.99 Kindle $8.95 softcover $15.95 hardcover**

The New Totalitarianism – Quo Vadis?

The previous century was one of the bloodiest in history. Two World Wars and many other wars do not bode well for our century that is beginning to rival the previous in its bloodlust. If we look carefully, we find in the last century the philosophical roots of the present century. The philosophers of the last century are the philosophers of the present. https://amzn.to/3AMZNFC **$5.99 Kinde $10.95 softcover $25.95 hard cover**

A Call to Reason

Is it possible that the problems in the world are not caused by capitalism and rich people? Is it possible that anti-capitalism and anti-reason philosophies are nothing more than elaborate hoaxes designed to convince people to give up everything they have honestly earned and take it away from them? Is it possible they are caused by the re-distribution of capital to wasteful uses and the consequent destruction of jobs and affluence? https://amzn.to/3mVNrq5 **$5.99 Kindle $9.95 softcover $24.95 Hardcover**

Poems for the Stage

Poems for the Stage – A Story of Love
This dramatic presentation features poems found in Mr. Villegas's book Poetic Prose and Poetry. Some are also found in his book. https://amzn.to/3gSJctV $2.99 Kindle $5.95 softcover

Poems for the Stage – The Man at the Computer
This dramatic presentation is based upon poems from Mr. Villegas's book Poetic Prose and Poetry. Some of the poems have been slightly altered to reflect the internal story. Mr. Villegas's book Poetic Prose and Poetry can be found on Amazon.com. https://amzn.to/2R8zpFf $2.99 Kindle $5.95 softcover

More Books on Politics and History

A Boomer takes on the Far Left

I just learned something about myself – and it isn't very good. In fact, it is very bad. I learned that the opinions of Boomers don't matter any more. We are obsolete in this new age of new knowledge. Anything we think is unimportant and false. I don't think so. https://amzn.to/3tzNqtc $5.19 Kindle $10.95 softcover

Crushing the Alinsky Radicals

The worst enemy of individual rights today is a group of people I call the Alinsky Radicals. These people are now in charge of our culture and temporarily, in charge of government. They are associated, philosophically and politically, with the communists and fascists of the past. They are not your father's liberals. They are the direct descendants of dictators such as Stalin and Mao. In this book, I hope to convince you of the evil of the Alinsky Radicals and to provide the intellectual ammunition you need to eradicate them from society. https://amzn.to/3hbh9WN $3.49 Kindle $8.95 softcover

The Conservative's Dilemma

I wrote this book to ask some important questions about the conservative philosophy of altruism. https://amzn.to/3bfDQ8e $2.99 Kinde $6.95 softcover.

The Biggest Mistakes in History – 2008 to 2016

To be the Chief Executive of the greatest country in the world requires a leader with a great deal of knowledge, experience and reasoning ability. It requires having the very best minds as advisors, minds that the President can count on to give reasoned arguments and detailed knowledge about the important issues of the day. I think it takes a special ability to understand the principle of cause and effect concerning how government action impacts the lives of real people. https://amzn.to/3tDQ4OI $2.99 Kindle $10.95 softcover

Books on Politics and History

Dachau and Berlin in 1990

This booklet chronicles Mr. Villegas' thoughts during visits to Dachau and Berlin during 1990, disclosing my observations of milestones in German history, past and present, and relating those events to world happenings as they were unfolding at the time. I traveled throughout Germany for much of 1990 while on business. https://amzn.to/3ex578d $2.99 Kindle $6.95 softcover

What Harvard and Princeton Don't Want You to Know

The professors at Harvard and Princeton don't want you to know about the worst ideas in history. This is because they have been pawning these ideas off as true and profound. They have been using them to deceive and manipulate us for centuries. https://amzn.to/3farP5p $5.19 Kindle $9.95 softcover

Defending American Values

This book is made up of several chapters about American values and how they can be defended without a descent into the abyss of dictatorship. The book argues for individual rights and provides reasons why we should fight for them. https://amzn.to/3uMFq9L $3.99 Kinde $5.95 softcover.

Capitalism Doesn't Fail

How many times have we heard the old saw: "Capitalism has failed again" over the course of contemporary events? We heard it during the Great Depression of 1929 after Hoover had invoked tariffs and precipitated economic retaliation and a banking crisis. Along with this question usually came a statement to the effect, that "We can fix capitalism and make it even stronger by issuing economic controls or spending money to stimulate economic activity." https://amzn.to/3xZIAJ6 $4.19 Kindle $10.95 softcover

Books on Psychology and Virtue

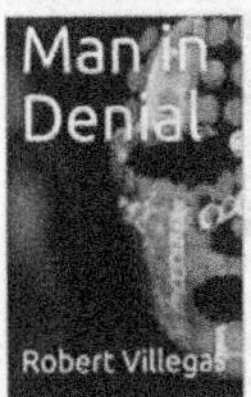

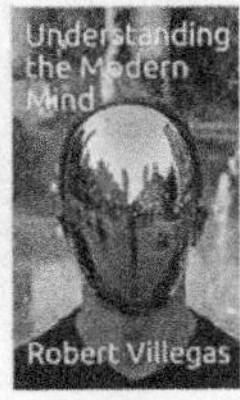

Naming Names in the NT

If psychology has no solid epistemology and metaphysics, how can it stand on its own? I do not think it can and this explains why psychology is in such a sad state today. Yet, before we can put psychology on a solid foundation, philosophy too must advance above the level of puberty. With its base in modern philosophy, even philosophy cannot stand on its own which exposes the real problems with modern psychology. https://amzn.to/3oVTDAQ **$5.99 Kindle $9.95 softcover $18.95 hardcover**

Finding Your Soft Cry

The purpose of this book is to delve into critical issues about how the human mind has come to the modern position of doubt and despair. The culprits in this matter include the irrationality of both rationalism and skepticism, and, in particular, the child of skepticism known as pragmatism.
https://amzn.to/3mRLZF9 **$6.99 Kindle $9.60 softcover $26.95 hardcover**

The New Totalitarianism – Quo Vadis?

One of the fathers of critical theory was Herbert Marcuse who escaped European dictatorship only by coming to America. America gave him the freedom and protection he needed to destroy capitalism in America.
https://amzn.to/2YW9LaS **$4.99 Kinde $8.95 softcover**.

A Call to Reason

A logical fallacy is a faulty thought process that violates a rule of proper thinking. Correct arguments are defined as proper generalized expressions that define logical truths or knowledge. In effect, a rule of logical reasoning addresses all of the common modes of valid argument while the faulty argument contradicts them. This book examines altruism as a logical fallacy.
https://amzn.to/3vdFiB0 **$5.99 Kindle $9.95 softcover $18.95 Hardcover**

Books on Sport and Entertainment Sponsorship

Finding Sponsors 1 and 2

This book is written for anyone seeking sponsorship relationships in the sport and entertainment fields. The ideas and principles presented here are applicable to any company, sport team, entertainment company, marketing agency and charitable organization that uses corporate sponsorships to support its activities. Volume 1: https://amzn.to/3ejm1Hp $5.19 Kindle $12.95 softcover Volume 2: https://amzn.to/3eVDo0e $4.69 Kindle $10.95 softcover

How to Write a Sponsorship Proposal

This booklet provide you with some basic guidelines on what to communicate in order to produce a winning sponsorship proposal. These guidelines will focus on what you should be presenting to your potential sponsor to make the best business case for involvement with your team or entertainment company. https://amzn.to/3tpHRxs $2.99 Kindle $6.95 softcover

Hospitality Event Planning Handbook

One key part of your sponsorship activation strategy might be customer hospitality events in conjunction with sporting events. How do you pull off a Hospitality Event for your biggest customers? You may not know how to start, what to do and how to ensure the event is a success. This book can help. http://amzn.to/2mxzpgy $7.95 softcover.

Selling Sponsorship in the Age of the Coronavirus

This book provides suggestions on how sport teams, athletes and concert promoters can mitigate the damage done to their businesses by the economic lockdowns (due to the Coronavirus). It integrates checklists, SWOT Analysis and other valuable business aids into one toolkit that will help you keep your sport and/or genre alive in these difficult times. https://amzn.to/2QVBNiM $5.15 Kindle $5.95 softcover

Books on Sponsorship and Business

Finding Sponsors Forms Book

This "Forms Book" is intended to provide samples of the forms mentioned in my book "Finding Sponsors for Sport and Entertainment". This will make it possible for you to reproduce these forms in other formats as well as download the forms document from the SponsorProAZ website for use with Microsoft Word. https://amzn.to/3b95yDW $2.99 Kindle $5.50 softcover

Submitting Your Sponsorship Proposal Online

This booklet enables sport teams and concert promoters to submit their sponsorship proposals to companies that accept only online submission of proposals. https://amzn.to/3euzdti $2.99 Kindle $5.95 softcover

The Art of Sponsorship

This short book is based upon Mr. Villegas' book "Finding Sponsors for Sport and Entertainment". It is also based upon a course that he taught for an organization managing Indiana Parks and Recreation facilities. It is, in a sense, a condensation of information from the book geared toward organizations that would like to earn revenues on their facilities through corporate sponsorship. https://amzn.to/3beuVnC $2.99 Kinde $6.95 softcover.

Restarting Your Business After the Pandemic

This new book is designed to help you restart your business after the Coronavirus pandemic. You will find here all the right questions, how you can find the answers and the forms you need to walk through your restart and coming success. https://amzn.to/2QVBNiM $5.15 Kindle $5.95 softcover

Made in the USA
Monee, IL
10 March 2024

54773139R00115